CALUMET THEATRE

ISBN: 0-942 363-13-2

Copyright Number: TX 345-214

Fourteenth of a Local History Series

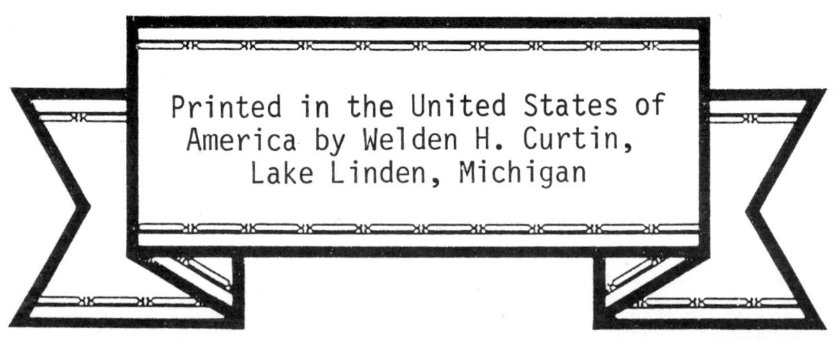

The cover picture was taken by Jay E. Dupuis of Lake Linden. If you are confused by the cover titles, both spellings are correct. The building was named the "Calumet Theatre," however, the sign says "Calumet Theater." It can be spelt either way.

AUTHOR'S NOTE

The data from which this book was compiled were secured through numerous sources. From the many conflicting statements which appear in the original manuscripts and newspapers, this author has chosen the data and incidents which appealed to his reason, after all possible research, as being most accurate. If any errors are detected or important information missing, please contact me. These entries are a combination of many sources, most of which are listed at the end of this compilation.

Sincerely,

Clarence J. Monette
Author

The headlines read "Blaze of Glory" and "New Theatre Opened for the First Time Last Evening." On March 20th, 1900, the Calumet Theatre was born with the presentation of the romantic comic opera "The Highwayman." This was the only municipal theatre in the United States of America and was owned by the village of Red Jacket, now known as Calumet. The manager chose for the scene of the first-night performance the Broadway Opera Company playing "The Highwayman," presented by Reginald De Koven and Harry B. Smith. According to an ad published in the Copper Country Evening News on Tuesday, March 20th, 1900, Manager John D. Cuddihy advertised that the tickets for the grand opening of the New Opera House would sell for $2.50, $2.00, and $1.00, with box seats going for $25.00 each. The net proceeds of the entertainment were to go to the Village of Red Jacket, to be applied to the first year's interest on the town hall and opera house bonds. Tickets were sold at the City Drug Store, Calumet, and Barry's Drug Store, Houghton.[1]

The house was filled to capacity, with twelve hundred people seeing the opening performance. Only a few vacant seats existed, those being the wooden benches in the top gallery, as might have been expected from the type of entertainment offered and the low prices of the tickets. The audience was, according to the opera company, an "ideal" one, as the management stated that the people appreciated the music. The opening of the new theatre had been looked forward to as an important society event, and the first night was decidedly a "dress" affair. The theatre patrons from all over copperdom were attracted to the brilliant electric sign of the Calumet Theatre, and the women of fashion seemed to feel that they were being less worldly by wearing, during the Lenten season, more modest theatre dresses than usual during such occasions. The people there represented the wealth, beauty, culture, and refinement of not only Red Jacket, but of the entire copper district.

The audience began to fill the building long before the announced time of the first performance. The patrons arrived early so that they could have an opportunity to look about and admire the details of decoration, furnishings, and lighting. No one was disappointed. The grand proscenium arch, rivaling in beauty of contour and depth that in any theatre in the whole country, was the first to attract attention. Upon the graceful curve of this arch were pictures representing "the arts." Viewing from left to right, they represented: "painting," "music," "drama," "poetry," and "sculpture." Away up in the vaulted ceiling was a copper spheroid with its hundred lights, and many a neck was craned to get a look at its dazzling brilliancy.[2] The Opera House Committee, consisting of John B. Vertin, Michael Kemp, and Thomas Gribbel, had worked many hours to make this theatre a dream come true.

The new theatre in its entirety was someting exceptionally elaborate for this section of the country. Previous to the first night, the auditorium had been repeatedly viewed by many people from many different angles and under various circumstances, but with the blaze of hundreds of electric lights and the animated effect produced by the gaiety in the audience, the scene was altogether one that was long to be remembered.[3]

It was a little late when the curtain went up on the first act of "The Highwayman," as the train with the crowd of Portage Lake people aboard was late in reaching Calumet. Special trains were run from Houghton and Hancock, returning after the performance. Before the curtain rose, President John

The Calumet Theatre, courtesy of Mrs. Gloria Coello, Manager of the Theatre.

R. Ryan, the head of Red Jacket's Common Council under whose direction the new building was completed, stepped up on the stage. He stated that he thought it would be fitting and proper at the opening of the new play house to hear an expression from someone who represented the interests surrounding the municipality, and upon which the village depended in a great measure for its support. He knew of no one present who represented those interests better than William E. Parnall, superintendent of the Bigelow Mines.

Mr. Parnall, in a few nicely chosen words, stated that he thought the new theatre would be a lasting benefit for the city. He also spoke of the good that was done by excellent plays, and that he thought the management intended having such dedicated persons on the boards that they could not do anything but add to the improvements that the village had vested in their new theatre. In closing he said that he did not see how the theatre, which he said was perfect in all its appointments, could have been built for the price. He was applauded by the huge audience as he closed.

The play was excellent, and the patrons were surprised when when during one feature of the play, a real horse appeared on the stage during the stage coach scene when the hold-up took place. This pleased the entire audience. The music was under the direction of Anton Heindi, and the Calumet & Hecla Mining Company orchestra performed it in exceptionally good style. The management of "The Highwayman" company informed a reporter that the music furnished for their production was exceptionally good, and the company's director opened his eyes and ears when he saw how well the Calumet & Hecla Mining Company orchestra handled his music with but one rehearsal. He said it was

Two boxes are located on each side of the stage.
Courtesy of Jay E. Dupuis, Lake Linden, Michigan

a pleasure to find an orchestra with such good musicians when on the road and stated that it compared favorably with what they had been running against in the largest cities. The music furnished between acts was also well rendered and well received by the audience.

After the performance S. T. King, the business manager of the Broadway Opera Company, was interviewed by a reporter for the Copper Country Evening News and was asked for his opinion of the Calumet Theatre. "It's a little gem," he said. "Its appointments are perfect, and there isn't anything better in the northwest. That's my honest opinion. There are larger houses, but nothing that strikes me as being an improvement on this." "You see," continued Mr. King, "we show how people look as much behind the curtain as in front of it. Most new theatres are built to please what the audience sees entirely, and the poor actors have to take chances on clumsy arrangements behind the footlights, but I have never seen any theatre with better or more convenient arrangements back of the drop curtain than you have right here in Calumet. It is certainly a beauty and you should feel proud of it." Mr. King had been in the theatrical business managing troupes for years and had traveled all over the United States and Canada; he was therefore in a position to know whereof he spoke.[4]

This news article further detailed the description of the new theatre as it was completed in March of 1900. Every detail of the work connected with the new building was done in a clever and artistic manner, and the contractors credited themselves for what was done in the new theatre. The work of the decorators and the electric lighting was more in evidence to the audience than anything else and was highly complimented. The theatre contained 1,441 incandescent lights, of which 275 were on the

12

RICHARD MANSFIELD as PRINCE KARL, CYRANO DE BERGERAC and BEAU BRUMMELL

proscenium arch, while 160 lights were used outside to spell out the name of the theatre.[5] A copper spheroid-shaped chandelier, brilliantly illuminated with over a hundred lights, was suspended from the vaulted ceiling. This copper chandelier was the pride of early theatre audiences.

The entrance to the theatre is from the sidewalk on Sixth Street. Across the walk is a porte cochere. This leads to the foyer, which has grained ceilings. The main entrance leads to the parquet circle of the theatre, and on either side of the entrance are marble stairways which lead to the family circle and the upper gallery. The floors were covered with green velvet Brussels carpet.

A gradual five-foot fall in floor elevation from the rear to the orchestra pit was achieved by a tier arrangement of seats. The aisles, however, were on a gradual continuous slope. Opera chairs of the latest design, upholstered in green Waldorf tapestry, were furnished by the Heywood Manufacturing Company of Chicago. William Eckert, also of Chicago, was awarded a contract for the interior decorations of the theatre, exclusive of the scenery, for a sum of $2,680.00. The general color scheme he used was a pleasing combination of crimson, gold, and ivory. A general relief work in Louis XIV style ornamented the proscenium, the grills of the boxes and curving contour of the balcony and gallery. Portieres, valances, and draperies were in empire green. The whole, when completed, presented one of the finest interior decorations to be found in theatres anywhere on the American continent.

The stage was built with a view of accommodating the largest traveling performances, and it

This is the stage as seen from the second balcony. Courtesy of Jay E. Dupuis, Lake Linden, Michigan

can never be said that the new opera house had a performing company that was unable to use all their stage scenery because the stage was too small. Even the accommodations behind the curtain were ample. All of the dressing rooms had the latest improvements, with electric lighting, steam heating, lavatories, etc.

A trap-door arrangement on the stage floor served both utilitarian and dramatic ends. It provided elevator service for lowering wardrobe trunks and heavy equipment to the dressing and property rooms below the stage, and it was also the device for executing disappearing acts found in many of the plays performed during that period.

Howard Tuttle, scenic artist of Milwaukee, built and painted the elaborate stage scenery for which he received $3,000. Several of these ornate sets and drops may still be seen today. They exist in a remarkable state of preservation after seventy-nine years, gathering dust and memories in the darkened backstage area of a present-day movie theatre. Their ghostly presence speaks of glorious days, now long gone.

Previous to the opening of the Calumet Theatre, all entertainment in the vicinity was presented in the old opera house which had opened in 1887. The old Red Jacket Opera House was located in the second story of the Village Hall. Laurium's opera house was in the Italian Hall. Complaints about the facilities were as frequent as shows were infrequent. These opera houses were fine for use as dance halls, for wedding receptions, political rallies, concerts, lectures, and home-talent plays, but they were very inadequate for the first-class production of shows and plays.

There were a few shows in the early days, as

This picture shows the stage trap door as seen from the basement. Courtesy of Jay E. Dupuis, Lake Linden, Michigan

John E. Warner performed in Red Jacket (Calumet) in 1868 as a member of a troupe featuring John Dillon. He returned three years later in a minstrel show. Otis Bowers played at the opening night of the old Red Jacket Opera House in April of 1887, performing in the Beach and Bowers Minstrels. He returned to Calumet on March 29th, 1900. In the early days, relatively few theatrical troupes found their way to this region, and the opera houses were used primarily for local purposes.

The first traveling presentation was booked by Mr. Cuddihy and was staged in the old Washington School building. Numerous attractions appeared in the district and were played in old St. Patrick's Hall which was constructed in 1873.

The Calumet Theatre was also known as the Red Jacket Opera House. The Opera House was a product of the post-Civil War era, but few communities could afford such luxuries. Toward the close of the century this attitude slowly changed. Before this period, the theatre was not approved by many churches, and several protestant denominations exercised a much greater influence in public affairs and social life than they do now. Social gatherings, amusements, and entertainment had to have church sanction to succeed. Singing schools, spelling bees, lectures, temperance meetings, and even circuses were defended as being educational by the church, but the theatre was another thing to these church folks.

In the early 1900's, the theatre sponsored musical affairs, religious plays, pantomimes, and pagents. The more liberal churchmen gradually relaxed their opposition to theatricals, and the communities were beginning to be interested in "cultural" affairs. It was during this period

THE CALUMET THEATRE

Wednesday Eve. May 7.

First Presentation Here Of The Peerless American Drama

ARIZONA

BY AUGUSTUS THOMAS, ESQ.,
Author of "Alabama,' "In Mizzouri," Etc.

Precisely as given for 300 nights in New York, 200 nights in Chicago, now at the Adelphia Theatre, London, England.

"Best Play Seen On Broadway In a Generation"...N. Y. Sun.

Scenery and Costumes Designed by Frederic Remington.

New York Cast and Production Intact

Grace Elliston.	Donald Mitchell.
J. W. Cope.	Ada Craven
Grace Thorne.	Stanley Murphy.
Dustun Farmun.	Wm. Hazeltine
Frazer Coulter.	Ben D. Deane.
Frank Campeau.	Frank Boun
Alma Bradley.	Clement Kirby
Jane Bliss Taylor.	

Curtain Rises At 8:45 Sharp.

Order Carriages For 11;45 p. m.

Special train over Mineral Range R. R. and H. & C. R. R. from Dollar Bay, Houghton and Hancock.

Seat Sale Opens Monday at 2 p. m.

PRICES:

Parquette and First Two Rows of Circle	$1 50
Balance Parquette Circle	1 00
First Two Rows of Balcony	1 00
Balance of Balcony	75
Balcony Circle	50
Gallery	25
Box Seats	1 50

Obtained from the Copper Country Evening News, Calumet, MI, May 1, 1902 that the Calumet Opera House as a civil project was constructed.

The best description of how and why the theatre was founded can be found in "Boom Copper," by Angus Murdoch. Page 151 and part of 152 are hereby quoted for your information, courtesy of Roy W. Drier and Louis G. Koepel.

"It was in 1898, towards the end of still another prosperous year, that the village council of Red Jacket gathered to ponder a problem, which has seldom confronted any community anywhere. The Red Jacket solons faced a pleasant dilemma. It was up to them to figure out how to spend the community's money.

"Every year, Red Jacket saloonkeepers called at the village clerk's office and left behind upwards of $27,000. For all their vast thirst, the citizens seldom robbed, burgled, or killed one another; and the police force was practically an honorary body. The village had no need for a park—the company had already given one. The fire department was handsomely equipped, the village streets were paved and lighted, and the Copper Country had somehow escaped a yen for statues. Yet there was $50,000 in the village treasury, and so far no one had thought of a sensible way to spend it.

"Then up spoke a councilman who had been brought up in Boston. "What Red Jacket needs," said he, "is an opera house. This isn't a Klondike boom town."

"And he spoke the truth.

"Ed Hulbert's red pudding stone had built a young metropolis where, thirty years before, there

MARIE CAHILL in
"NANCY BROWN"

had been nothing but pine and Billy Royal's Half Way House. Sixty-six thousand people had come from half the world to mine and mill some of the richest vein rock the earth had ever disclosed.

"Thirty years has been the entire life span of most American mining camps. Many vanished before they outgrew their boom-town, dance-hall days. But here an ephemeral boom town had actually grown to manhood. It had butchers and bakers, merchants and chiefs. Now it was ready for culture.

"An opera house, the council concurred, was just what Red Jacket needed. The members were so enthusiastic that they telephoned C. K. Shand, Detroit's leading architect, that very night and commissioned him to draw up plans at once. It took a year to complete the tiresome details, but on March 20, 1900, a handsome three-story structure of native red sandstone was ready to seat eleven hundred of Calumet Township's upper crust. Those who were vulgar enough to mention the matter said the elegant structure cost $59,815.18.

"Red Jacket agreed that their councilmen had spent wisely, for in the next few years the greatest names of the theater trod the boards of their proud opera house."[5]

In 1900, Calumet boasted of having 45,000 people, and among the lot were 2,000 or 3,000 who claimed to love the drama and the opera but were denied the pleasure of seeing either dramas or operas of note because there was no play house wherein a company of standard reputation could be induced to appear. Now there was every probability that the higher-class performances would visit the city and would be liberally patronized also.

A view of the rear of the first floor. Courtesy of Mrs. Gloria Coello, Manager.

At the close of the nineteenth century, the Copper Country was not a traditional western mining camp but rather a permanent, solidly established community of good homes, excellent schools, and many churches. It also had a well-developed and stable economic life. Families from the second and third generations formed the base of the social stratum. Many people from Boston, Pittsburgh, and other cities in the East had arrived during the first copper boom in the 1840's, inspired by the geological findings of Douglass Houghton. They brought with them the capital which was to develop the resources of this region, as well as the know-how and the culture which was to maintain their way of life.

Now, at the turn of the century, there were many signs of prosperity and development in the Copper Country. Nearby towns were expanding their city limits, and two daily newspapers were published in the area. New hotels, homes, and even business blocks were being built. An electric railway which would bring these towns together through interurban service received its charter. Newspapers began advertising typewriters, telephones, and electric service. For the first time, the human voice was carried by long-distance telephone from the Copper Country to Detroit and Lansing. The outside world was beginning to realize that the Copper Country had some of the luxuries of modern civilization.

The second performance at the new Red Jacket Opera House was held on the following evening, March 21st, 1900, with the play "Faust." If there was a large attendance at the opening of the new theatre, the crowd that was on hand for this next play was a record breaker in the history of the city. It was, beyond a doubt, the largest audience that had ever assembled in a playhouse in the Copper

The basement storeroom as seen by actors. Courtesy of Jay E. Dupuis of Lake Linden, Michigan

Country. Two days before the production, the sale of tickets had exhausted everything on the first floor and almost everything on the second. When the curtain went up, there wasn't a vacant seat anywhere, and even the standing room in the gallery was occupied.

This play was the immortal "Faust," presented by one of Louis Morrison's companies, but it was not Morrison himself who played the part of Mephisto. Critics said that as a whole, the production was not anything of very exceptional merit, and many who had seen John Griffith in the same play were better pleased with his rendition of the character. The stage fixtures of the new theatre gave the company every opportunity to work this part of the drama to the limit, and the electrical display was excellent.

Many people in the audience had said that Morrison was the leading character, but that well-known man had not played the part for a year, and he had three companies on the road giving his dramatization of "Faust." The company at Calumet was one of them. The play had been presented in Calumet several times, and each time it had been good, so the Morrison company, of whom so much had been expected, was at a disadvantage. Although the audience did not get very enthusiastic, they appeared to enjoy the production.[7]

Advance publicity for this play stated that the manager, Porter J. White, carried 16,000 feet of electrical wire, eight calcium lights, and almost 20,000 square feet of scenery, all of which were to be seen in his production of "Faust." At this time many Copper Country residents were intrigued with the trappings of the play, even as the old Greeks were with their shows.

BLANCHE WALSH in
"THE WOMAN IN THE CASE"

Among the early employees of the theatre when it opened were Robert Haskell, Peter Pasquinelli, Laughlin McDonald, George Harvey, Dexter DuMonthier, Joseph Forester, Jr., Max Asselin, Fred Nordstrom, and Joseph Harris. Harris later became a player in stock and visited Calumet on numerous occasions. Those in charge of the front of the theatre were James Long, treasurer; Thomas Daniels, parquet doorman; and Walter Borgo, in charge of the balcony division. The ushers were John Kearns, James Meades, Albert Barrett, Christ Gribble, Evelyn Carter, and Ryan Gaul. Program passers in the parquet were John Gaul and William Forster. E. McKenna was the electrician. The first motion picture was shown at the Calumet Theatre in June 1903. The Calumet & Hecla Mining Company band also gave Sunday afternoon concerts in a type of matinee period.

Albert Burkman was the ticket seller, obtaining this position after he graduated from Calumet High School in 1901. Hired by the Village Clerk Albert Mertz, it was up to Albert Burkman to set up the board. He placed the tickets in the slots according to the manner in which the seating lay in the parquet and balcony. He had nothing to do with the gallery seats as they went on sale the day of the performance and could not be reserved. Not only did Albert dispose of the theatre tickets, but he collected village water fees and performed other such duties as now come under the scheme of managing the village form of government.

He worked on a personally paid salary tendered him by the village clerk. Things were busy in those days as the theatre catered only to road shows, and these arrived in town frequently during the whole year. The official ticket dispenser was W. S. Paddock, and it was he who sold the pasteboards on the evening of the performance.

The ticket seller's day began at 8:30 in the morning, and there was usually a large crowd waiting for his arrival. It did not take long to rid the house of its seat tickets. Usually, to avoid the crowd, Burkman would enter through a side door so that he would not have to contend with the advance patrons who were waiting for admission tickets. There was usually no trouble in handling the deluge once he got into the office for the first patron on hand got his choice of seats. Phone calls were not accepted in those days, so if one wanted tickets he had to present himself bodily.

Often a group would delegate a specific person to purchase the ducats. Calumet & Hecla Mining Company personnel did this, and so did the then existent Calumet & Hecla Hospital. For the latter, the assemblage purchaser usually was the late James Perry.[8]

According to a list of Red Jacket Opera House shows, the next big attraction was "Macbeth," with Madame Modjeska who had been long acknowledged as the greatest exponent of tragedy that the English-speaking stage had produced in that generation.

On December 3rd, 1900, the rush for seats for this presentation, when the sale commenced at the City Drug Store at 9:30 that morning, exceeded anything of that kind that had ever been seen in the city of Calumet. The interior of the drug store bore a decided resemblance to an auction room in a big city on bargain day, and the rush to get seats could not have been greater had Manager Cuddihy advertised free seats to all applicants with a Christmas souvenir thrown in.

The sale of seats was advertised to begin

promptly at 9:30 a.m. Some time before that hour came the expectant crowd began to gether in the drug store. When 9:30 came the crowd was so large that it was evident that there were not enough seats in the house to satisfy them, and another dilemma occurred in the fact that there would be a clamor for choice of seats. After a little consultation it was decided that the only fair method was to write numbers from 1 to 100 on separate slips of paper, shake them up in a hat and let the waiting crowd take turns in drawing from the hat. This was accordingly done. Then Messrs. Jerry Sullivan and Harry Reed began to dispence seats to the waiting crowd. There was quite a clamor to get up to the counter. Mr. Reed called off the numbers with "one" and the possessor of each number, as his name was called, crowded to the front, designated the seats he wanted, and retired to the rear.

It looked pretty dubious for those fellows whose numbers were way up in the 80's or 90's. No buyer was allowed more than eight seats. Many of the less fortunate possessors of high numbers began to do a little soliciting among those of their friends who had low numbers and who did not require eight seats for themselves. In that way many secured seats so that when Mr. Reed got up into the 60's, there were a good many blanks. In a little over an hour every seat in the house had been sold, with the exception of a number which had been reserved by request by a Houghton party which was coming out on a special train that evening.

Many people who were there when the sale started were unable to get seats at all. All that day there was a steady stream of applicants for seats at the drug store who had to be turned away because the house had been "sold out."[9]

The entrance to the theatre. Courtesy of Jay E. Dupuis, Lake Linden, Michigan

The production of "Macbeth" with its strong supporting company was undoubtedly the greatest theatrical event that had ever occurred in the Copper Country. The production was elaborately staged, was produced with infinite care, and was presented before one of the most brilliant audiences that had ever graced a performance in Upper Michigan. Suffice it to say that every seat in the theatre was occupied. A number of folding chairs were placed by order of Manager Cuddihy in the balcony and on the first floor where they would not obstruct free passage of the people to and from the doors in case there should be an alarm of any kind, and these seats were all occupied. The major portion of the costumes to be seen in the house were very elaborate. The section reserved for the Houghton visitors were filled with the delegation that came out from the Portage Lake towns, many of whom had never seen Red Jacket's new opera house, but who went home filled with admiration for it.

The Calumet & Hecla orchestra prepared an exceptionally fine musical program for the evening. The duet for the cornet and trombone by Messrs. Cowley and Harry King was received with applause, and the descriptive hunting scene by Bucalossi was greatly enjoyed by all in the audience who loved music.

About the play itself, it was hard to find words to do it justice. Although Modjeska had long since passed the median of life, and the marks of age had begun to show upon her features, she was never a more brilliant actress than she was during that play. In the metropolitan theatre where she had been playing, dramatic critics had pronounced her production of "Macbeth" the most elaborate of her whole repertoire.[10]

This area is located behind the rear row on the first floor. Courtesy of Jay E. Lake Linden, Michigan

During that same afternoon, the company presented "Mary Stuart" to a large audience. Modjeska, as the hapless Queen Mary, displayed her talent with grand effort. In the third act Elizabeth, Queen of England, and Mary meet in the part at Farthingay, and the scene was reported to be magnificent, as Elizabeth goes in her pride of regal beauty and power to gloat over the sufferings of her captured rival. The report goes on to explain the actors were excellent, and the costumes worn on the stage were very elaborate and rich. Much had been said and written about Madame Modjeska's advancing age, and while it had been admitted that the arduous and exacting work of the parts was rather extreme for her to attempt so late in her life, it was also admitted that she gave a magnificent portrayal of any character she assumed. Her dignity, finesse, and forcefulness which were so often talked about were clearly demonstrated.

Mr. James Louis was also noted, as he seemed quite superior to his former self to his many friends in the audience. His manly and dignified bearing coupled with his graceful, easy style and splendid voice united in winning for him the high esteem which his ability entitled him to.

A newspaper ad stated that there were two carloads of special scenery and fifty people, which was the most complete, sumptuous, and scholastic production ever shown in the city of Red Jacket.

Many people from Houghton and Hancock were seen in the audience. A special train was run from Dollar Bay and Portage Lake on that Thursday evening for the accommodation of those who wished to attend the performance. The train returned twenty minutes after the evening performance. The round-trip ticket sold for 50 cents, good for all day, thus

The theatre as seen from the stage. Courtesy of Jay E. Dupuis, Lake Linden, Michigan

giving the patron an opportunity to attend the afternoon matinee or do some shopping.[11]

The Red Jacket Opera House had been built without a basic safety feature, namely a fire escape. The management had felt secure in the fact that the theatre had two staircases leading to the balcony and gallery, which could be emptied in seven minutes should a disaster occur. However, the pressures of public sentiment forced the Red Jacket Village Council to install a fire escape on one side in 1901.

John Philip Sousa was a big name in March of 1902 and is still well known. When Colonel George Frederic Hinton, who was Mr. Sousa's representative, visited Red Jacket on Saturday, March 2, 1902, he made arrangements for the appearance of the band to play at the Opera House on Saturday, March 15th. Mr. Hinton was still enthusiastic over the success Sousa and his band had had during their last trip to Europe. The cable reports had told the story of Sousa's triumphs in Great Britain and of his concert before the King, and it was a great satisfaction to add that the financial returns of the trip were almost as great as the popular and artistic success of the American musicians.

Saturday, March 15, 1902, finally arrived, and John Philip Sousa and his famous band was greeted at the Calumet Theatre by two audiences that broke all records in point of numbers and enthusiasm than had ever gathered in that house. Many people who would have liked to hear the March King and his organization were unable to secure seats. Others who were unable to procure seats crowded into the theatre and occupied chairs in aisles or remained standing throughout the entire concert.

HARRY
HOUDINI

The entertainment was said to be wonderful. Each number produced great applause, and it was the general verdict that the music was superb, superior to anything ever heard in Calumet. One feature which pleased the people in general was the fact that the program was not confined to the classics. It was a program arranged to please everybody, and that it did. One article stated that it did not matter whether it was a classic, a march, or just a melody, as the performance of the music was something out of the ordinary, and each selection was rendered in a polished manner.

Exquisite skill was also shown in the solo numbers, each being rendered with as perfect a technique and tone as the most critical might wish, while the perfect control of the leader over his band was a revelation to those who had never before seen him. It seemed as though he had every instrument at his fingers' end and could control them at will. He was noted as a wonderful conductor, and he had with him a most wonderful band. When one had heard him, it left no doubt as to why he had enjoyed such success in Europe. The music rolled out as from an immense organ manipulated by other than human fingers.

Aside from the 50 members of the band, Miss Maud Reese-Davis, soprano, and Miss Dorothy Hoyle, violinist, did their share to make the evening enjoyable. The young lady singer possessed a sweet voice, highly cultivated, and splendidly controlled, and she sang with perfect ease the difficult sections assigned to her. As a violin artist, Miss Hoyle possessed an extraordinary ability, her work stamping her as master of the king of musical instruments. In addition, Arthur Pryor, trombone soloist, delighted his audience.[12]

Calumet was very fortunate to obtain two

performances, for in the rapid tour that the band was making, they usually stopped but a few hours at each point. They spared only one day for St. Paul-Mineapolis, playing one city for the matinee and the other in the evening. His famous band returned to Calumet in 1906 and again in 1912 to please the local residents.

For those two performances, two special trains were run over the Mineral Range railway for the benefit of the Torch Lake and Dollar Bay people who desired to attend the entertainment. The train from Dollar Bay left at 7 o'clock and from Lake Linden at 7:30. The returning special trains left Calumet 20 minutes after the close of the show, running via the mills route. Fifty cents for the round-trip rail ticket was charged.

Two years later, Calumet's main entertainment rendezvous was given a companion, as in 1902 the Kerredge Theatre formally opened its doors to the public. The two, throughout the years of musical comedies, operas, and dramatic stage shows formed an interesting duo to presenting companies. The touring troupes always liked the Copper Country assignment because it meant two houses close to one another. Usually a stage show would hit Calumet or Hancock and then the other the next evening. This meant for easy moves and gave the troupes a brief respite from one-night stands. All traveling, of course, was done by trains with the scenery and stage paraphernalia going ahead in a baggage car.

Although designed primarily for theatrical performances, the Calumet Theatre was also used for lectures, lyceum presentations, commencement exercises, and similar community enterprises. In 1904 lecturers who spoke there included many such widely different personalities as the noted sculptor Lorado Taft, America's foremost welfare worker Jane Addams, and socialist Eugene Debs. Since the theatre was a municipal institution, it was available for all types of entertainment approved by the City Council for a fee of $40.00 per night.

The immortal Sarah Bernhardt arrived in the Copper Country area in May of 1911, playing at the Calumet and Kerredge Theatres. At the time of her billing at Calumet, she was 65 years of age, having been born in Paris on October 22, 1845. It was a special train that brought the renowned European satelite to the Keweenaw Peninsula. The first play date was in Calumet, and because of this, when her train arrived in the early morning, there was a throng to witness the Mineral Range engines pull her car up the Hancock hill from the bridge to the Boston region. The Franklin Mine as well as the Quincy Mine was working at the time, and especially at the Hancock depot there were many people on hand to witness the arrival of her dramatic majesty.

At the Calumet Theatre on May 30, she appeared in "Camille," whereas at the Kerrege in Hancock the next evening, her offering was "L'Aiglon." This was the touching story of the young duke of Relchstadt, son of Napoleon I, who, when the play opened in 1830, was living at Baden with his mother Maria Louisa, second wife of Napoleon I and widow of Count Nelpperg. The play exposes a plot to abduct the youthful prisoner, on whom the eyes of Europe rested so anxiously.[14]

Sarah Bernhardt appeared in Calumet for the first time to act in one of her greatest plays, "Camille," which was held before a very large audience. She captured and entranced her audience who, upon her first appearance on the stage,

"SARAH BERNHARDT"

immediately lost all sight of her name and fame and became enraptured by her pure, beautiful acting. Although Bernhardt and her original Paris company gave "Camille" in the original French, every word, almost every idea and phrase was thoroughly understood because of the perfect acting.

As one went timidly to the performance of "Camille," the feeling toward this wonderful French woman was mixed with homage. In this great love play, there were many amorous pleading scenes into which even genius might fear to jump if unaccompanied by the graces of youth. A touch of the ridiculous here would have more than destroyed the illusion of the evening.

All of these fears were unnecessary, however, so vital was the spirit of this woman, so possessed with the undying enthusiasm of youth, so tender her charm, so wistful her grace, that never for a moment did the love-making of an Armand, who was younger than most Armands, seem ridiculous or out of place.

The show was a tremendous success and was filled with emotion.[15] Incidentally, the prices for Sarah's Calumet Theatre performance were three dollars for the parquet, two dollars for the balcony, and one dollar for the gallery. Box seats were also three dollars.

While she was in the Copper Country, Sarah Bernhardt made a trip down into the low recesses of the Quincy Mine, and it was reported that she enjoyed her experience immensely. Mr. Louis J. Van Hoff was the chauffeur for this famed actress. It seems that he was employed by the Northern Garage, and the garage officials dispatched him with a car to chauffeur the actress wherever she

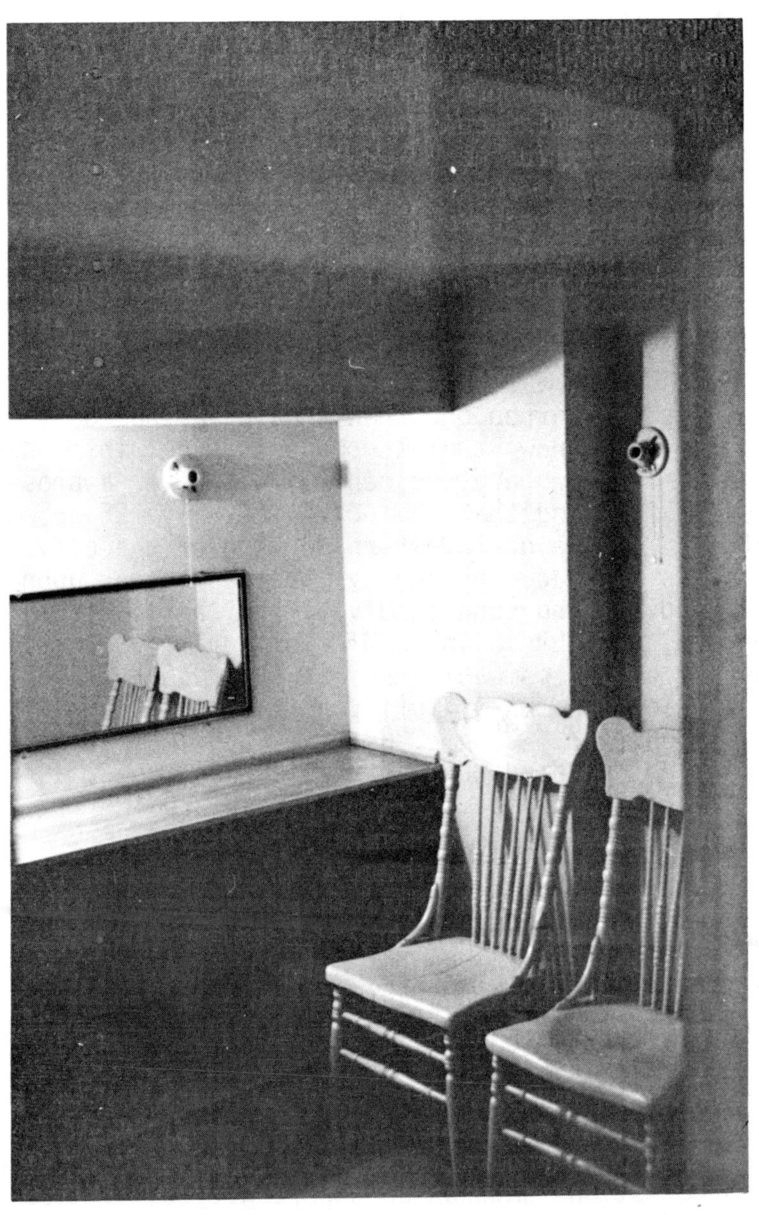

One of the dressing rooms in the basement of the theatre. Courtesy of Jay E. Dupuis, Lake Linden, Michigan

might wish to travel. At this time, the garage was owned by John Funkey and Ernest Hansen. Dr. J. E. Scallon was the interpreter who traveled with the famed Copper Country visiting party, as the "divine" Sarah seemed unfamiliar with the English language. Dr. Scallon was an Irishman who could speak French better than some of the French people in the village.

Van Hoff recalls that during the trip through Quincy's Mine, the physician did not go down into the mine with Sarah but remained on the surface until she returned and then completed the tour. It was well known that the Hancock Mine, into which shaft Miss Bernhardt descended, was never a prosperous firm and that it controlled only 725 acres of land in the northwestern portion of the city. She was also accompanied by Theatre Manager John D. Cuddihy, who suggested visiting the mine; Dr. Marote, her physician; a Mr. Tellegram, who was a member of the company; Madame Ceylor, her traveling companion; and E. J. Sullivan, manager of her American tour. John L. Harris, Superintendent of the mine, piloted the party while Roy Heber, a local photographer, snapped the pictures.

This mine trip was made after she dined in her special car which remained at the Mineral Range Depot. At 2 p.m. Bernhardt arrived at the mine in a heavy fur coat and purple hat. The descent into the mine was made in the big Kimberly Skip at a rapid rate, although not as fast as the skip usually travels. On the thirteenth level, the party was put aboard an electric car which had been specially upholstered and cushioned for the party of the divine Sarah. Underground, she asked many questions and had an opportunity to witness the actual work of drilling. After the trip, she expressed herself as having been greatly delighted with the experience and said it was one of the

These stairs lead to the first and second balconys, however, only the first is in use. Courtesy of Jay E. Dupuis, Lake Linden, Michigan

most enjoyable in her career. The descent was made in the number 2 shaft, and much has been said about the fanfare attached to the trip.

Both the Kerredge and Calumet Theatres were sellouts for her appearances. When she departed from the district, it was to go south to Milwaukee for additional appearances in the "Cream City."[17]

As the first decade melted into the second, bookings became fewer and fewer. The records for the years 1913 - 1920 are missing; the theatre, however, did not close, and its activities can be pieced together from newspaper accounts during this period. The kinodromes, shown originally as curiosities, grew up to become movies. In the 1920's, the theatre showed classics such as "Little Annie Rooney," "Birth of a Nation," and "Phantom at the Opera."

The talk of the town during the early part of January 1916 was "The Golden Ball" which was presented by a large company and was produced under the auspices of the Calumet Elks. The local entertainers performed at the Calumet Theatre on January 13th and 14th, and the presentation was one of unusual merit. Frequent rehearsals were held to insure its presentation in a finished, perfect manner. Credit for the creation of "The Golden Ball" was due two Calumet ladies: Mrs. Lucy K. Been who originated the plot for the clever fantasy, and Mrs. Ruth D. Engstrom who wrote the music. The orchestration had been arranged by Director Clarence E. Cook of the Calumet & Hecla Mining Company band.

It was a big, juvenile musical fantasy, and the seat sale for the two performances were unusually heavy as capacity audiences clamored for the advance reservations. The cast numbered 147 people, ranging from tiny tots to grown-ups, drilled entirely by Mrs. Lucy Kneeland Been who wrote the play. The play was built around a delightful little story, every detail of which had been cleverly developed, and the careful selection of the cast tended to make the production the best of the season. Reporters wrote that this play was one of the happiest and liveliest combinations of laughter, song, and dance that had ever been seen in Calumet that season.[18]

A heavy demand for reservations for the Forbes-Robertson engagement was also experienced at the opening of the seat sale at Forster's Newsstand in Calumet on the morning of January 15th, 1916. Theatre patrons were eager to see the famed English actor and his company of stars. Lines of people were on hand long before the ticket counter opened, and by 8 o'clock the line extended for half a block. The advance sale for the matinee performance "Hamlet" also went on sale.

This was the first and last opportunity that Calumet Theatre patrons would have to see the distinguished English actor, as this was his farewell tour of America. The privilege of seeing so great an artist was one seldom afforded the Copper Country, and the two large opera houses greeted the celebrated dramatist. In the afternoon performance of "Hamlet," Forbes-Robertson presented a clear-cut, intellectual treat that bestowed the keen pleasure that perfect artistry gives in "The Passing of the Third Floor Back." For the evening performance, he made a direct appeal to the heart in a sermon on love and kindness, pleasantly coated with sentiment.

It was in "Hamlet" that his art stood out most prominently because of the great opportunity for emotional acting. Here he clearly demonstrated he was the Hamlet of the genius in "The Passing of the

Third Floor Back." The evening's presentation was an abrupt transition in that it did not demand the powerful acting the Shakespearean piece required, but in both performances his fine presence, his beautiful voice, and his indisputable genius were ever present as he held his audiences spellbound. A critic said that the performance of every member of the cast was admirable, the rapid succession of scenes and situations and the magnetism of the players inspiring the audience with the belief that Forbes-Robertson's Hamlet correctly interpreted the conception of Shakespeare.[19]

Copper Country theatre-goers had the pleasure of greeting the San Carlo Grand Opera Company in February of 1918. They were returning to Calumet for their second engagement, and the greeting they received was more than cordial, and there was plenty of reason for appreciation. The Company had materially improved during the past year, and the patrons had never enjoyed a better performance than they did on February 18th when "Faust" was presented during the afternoon. At the evening performance, the offering was a double billing—"Cavalleria Rusticana" and "Pagliacci." The chorus was somewhat larger than it had been the past year, and it had gained in balance and in the quality of its ensemble.

According to a local newspaper article, the presentation of "Cavalleria Rusticana" was altogether delightful. Praise was heaped on the principals Luisa Darclee, Miss Marta Melis, Alice Homer, and several others in the company. Several paragraphs were allocated to the superb orchestra, as it was reported that the orchestra was a well-balanced organization and was admirably directed by Carlo Peroni. Also drawing praise was the promptness with which the performances were started and the quickness of the various changes

A picture of the bell which is maintained on the side of the theatre. Courtesy of Jay E. Dupuis, Lake Linden, Michigan

of shows. It proved that the management was capable and had taken the audience and its aversion to tedious delays into consideration. There were no long waits, and the action proceeded with smoothness and dispatch.[20]

In these early days of the Calumet Theatre, the Copper Range Hotel was also well known and was associated with the theatre. This hostelry catered extensively to the acting groups at the show house and even more so to the crowds which attended the performances. It had a flash system informing playgoers of the beginning and end of the acts which helped the management and staff of the hotel to provide the proper type of refreshments. Liquid refreshments and a sandwich or two were in demand between the acts. The Copper Range Hotel was located directly north of the theatre and was owned for a long time by Dominic Vairo who also ran the establishment as a boarding house. Many of the most celebrated performers of the day used its facilities.

The "Sunshine Lady," a musical play produced by LeCorate and Flasher, was declared a snappy play by the patrons in September of 1919. This theatre company, which made a formal bow to Copper Country theatre patrons on the 22nd of September, provided that evening one of the most delightful concoctions that had been brought to the Calumet Theatre for several seasons. In the first place, the title was not a misnomer, for the piece fairly bristled with the bright, timely comedy and the elaborate settings and costumes which contributed so much to the show's success.

The chorus was comely, as a whole, and the dancers were clever. Combined with the dancing were numerous song hits; particularly enjoyed were "My Sunshine Lady," "I Believe in Fairies," and

"Love of Mine," all of which were well performed. A critic went on to say that "contrary to most musical shows, there was a clever little plot in "My Sunshine Lady" which is introduced in the Prologue and is sustained throughout the production."[21]

In 1919 the Calumet Theatre had another thrill, but far different from any other because it was not held inside the theatre. It seems that "Sailor Jack," known the country over at that time as "The Human Fly," thrilled more than 2,000 Calumet people during the afternoon of September 29th when he scaled the front of the Red Jacket Theatre building. Without the aid of ropes or ladders, he climbed to the top of the flag staff. For sheer daring and fearlessness, Sailor Jack probably had no equal, and the crowd of people who stood almost breathless as he performed his seemingly impossible feat could testify that he had more downright nerve than any man who ever had appeared before in the Copper Country.

He chose for his starting point the wall near the entrance to the town hall. By grasping projections—anything that would afford a finger hold—he worked his way upward, clinging here and there to ornamental stone or window ledges, all the while glancing down at the crowd and exchanging bits of repartee with the spectators. On corners where there were no ornaments or protruding bricks, he simply shinned up the bricks with the same ease that an ordinary mortal would ascend a stairs. As he approached the tower in which the municipal clock is located, he perched upon a little ornamental stone sphere and whirled himself around while the crowd stood agape. Probably more than half the people who watched his antics by this time dropped their eyes, fearful that he would miss or his grip would loosen and the "human fly" would come tumbling down to the pavement. The other half stood aparently transfixed as he caught hold of the ropes of the flag staff and pulled himself up.

Halfway up the staff he injected a few more death-defying stunts into his exhibition by winding his legs about the slender pole and throwing his body backward and sideways, just to convince the spectators that there was no limit to his daring. His descent was almost as thrilling as the ascent, and the crowd sighed with relief as he stepped to the ground.

Sailor Jack had come to the Calumet District a week before and was working for the Calumet & Hecla Mining Company as a trammer, giving the mining company his name as Smith. It seems that he had been employed that summer on the Great Lakes, but the sympathetic strike of the sailors had left him marooned in the Copper Country.

Smith was to do a repeat performance the next day at 7 p.m. when he would again climb the theatre building tower, but under a spot light. The Ahmeek Military Band furnished the music during the exhibition. On Monday evening he was to climb the town hall building in Lake Linden, and on Wednesday evening he thrilled the Houghton people by climbing the walls of the Douglass House Hotel.[22]

Noted Finnish artists appeared at the Calumet Theatre on April 24th, 1921. Selim Palmgren, the Chopin of the North, was joined in the recital by his wife, Makki Jernefelt. He had received a good education and had graduated from the University of Helsing with a bachelor of arts. There was no pianist of greater appeal to music lovers than Palmgren, and the interest in his works was intense among the many persons who looked forward to hearing

CHAUNCEY OLCOTT in
"A ROMANCE of ATHLONE"

his own interpretation of the compositions that so rapidly made him famous. Nearly all of his piano works had been published in the United States. The husband and wife team appeared in New York under the auspices of the Metropolitan Concert Company, scoring a definite hit with their audience. They later appeared in Minneapolis and the music department of the University of Minnesota.[23]

The Calumet Theatre celebrated its twenty-fifth birthday during the month of February 1925. This event was celebrated by engaging the Beach-Jones Stock Company to provide a week of entertainment. The company stood out as being the leader in repertoire that season. Two special railroad cars carried the scenery and equipment for the troupe. Billed as "Anniversary Week at the Calumet Theatre," the production "Those Who Dance," a gripping drama of the underworld, was the Sunday special, with shows at 2:30, 7:00, and 8:30 p.m. Other plays included "The Little Red Head," "The Mad Honeymoon" (a melodramatic comedy) "Little Old New York," "Potash and Perlmutter," "Sweet 17," "The Woman on the Jury," and "Our New Minister."[24]

John Weicher, assistant conductor of the Chicago Symphony Orchestra, scored brilliantly on Thursday, March 2, 1935, when he and the Calumet orchestra closed its 1934-1935 season before a large and appreciative audience at the Calumet Theatre. Mr. Weicher had returned to Calumet as guest soloist for the second time, and this triumph was a repetition of the enthusiastic reception he had received the year before. He had been invited back because of his flawless technique, his modesty, and his great sincerity which made his performance something quite personal, quite rare, and quite winning.

A view of the first balcony. Courtesy of Jay E. Dupuis, Lake Linden, Mich

Much of the applause went to Arthur E. Kitti for his capable direction, and to the orchestra which again displayed the remarkable degree of perfection that it had attained under its popular director. The fine spirit which reigned among Mr. Kitti's musicians was one of the most prominent elements in the symphony's personality, and the results were a fitting tribute to Mr. Kitti and the members of the organization. Its success, in which the director no doubt took a personal and pardonable pride, had been well earned, if only for what it had brought to the Copper Country music lovers since its organization.

In addition to Mr. Weicher's solo numbers, the orchestra provided selections for the balance of the program and proved popular and thoroughly enjoyable. It also allowed the conductor ample opportunity to bring out the excellent talent and great possibilities of his orchestra. The audience included 50 delegates to the Fifth Annual Convention of the Houghton District of the Michigan Federation of Music Clubs which had opened their convention in Calumet that day.[25]

The theatre was now known as a movie theater, for this was what the patrons wanted. Operas were more cherished during the years of 1900 to 1920, and many of the Calumet and Kerredge opera fans delighted in the appearances of the San Carlo and DeKoven Opera Companies when they had traveled northward in those early days. In addition to the Boston-English Company, these "long hair" producers of music roles a la class tallied up to some of the most renowned cultural offerings ever to be brought to the 15 counties north of the Wisconsin border. The DeKoven Company presented "Robin Hood" with Ralph Dunbar. Reginald DeKoven gave forth with the music while the libretto was the work of Harry B. Smith.

MAUDE ADAMS
AND SCENES FROM "PETER PAN"

With the frequent appearance of the highly admired musical comedies, an offering like the DeKoven Company or the San Carlo was greatly appreciated. The 1954 generation was unable to remotely speculate as to the excellence of the shows brought to the Upper Michigan Territory in days after the construction of the Red Jacket and Kerredge Theatres. The same offerings showing in the Copper Country also appeared in Sault Ste. Marie, Escanaba, Marquette, Menominee, and Ironwood areas.

Scores of Keweenaw Peninsula people could recall with considerable pleasure the Marquette Opera House. It contained a glorious maze of seating tiers and dressing rooms with the characteristic small framing light bulbs around the mirrors, and it ranked high in actual-presence exhibition rendezvous.

Frequently casts from New York toured the North country. Many of the shows played locally before going on the big-city stage for extended runs. This gave the Upper Peninsula audiences a first glimpse of some of the most renowned players of the day, for many of the companies brought the regular cast which played such cities as Milwaukee, Detroit, Minneapolis, and St. Paul. The first two decades after the turn of the century were great periods in stage performances. In many respects, those years might well be termed the golden age in the annals of the Upper Peninsula theatre.[26]

The Keweenaw Playhouse saw its beginnings in 1958. Based in the historic Calumet Theatre, its second season opened in June of 1959 with Paul G. Berry being the producer and president of the Keweenaw Playhouse, Inc. Barry had spent much of his time that winter lining up the professional actors, production crew, and apprentices who would

A picture of the first and second balconys.
Courtesy of Jay E. Dupuis, Lake Linden, Michigan

help stage the ten plays that were scheduled for Upper Michigan's only professional summer stock theatre. They opened the season with "No Time for Sergeants." Other productions staged that season were "Of Mice and Men," "Diary of Anne Frank," "Blithe Spirit," "Midsummer Night's Dream," "Cat on a Hot Tin Roof," "The Matchmaker," "Picnic," "The Emperor Jones," and "Voice of the Turtle."

The Keweenaw Playhouse brought live professional theatre back to the Copper Country for the first time in more than 30 years when it opened for the season in 1958. Barry, a New York and Hollywood actor, a Michigan native and graduate of Wayne University, had for several years considered opening a summer stock theatre. Early in 1958 he made a study of existing summer companies and was surprised that of the 350 in the United States, none was located in Michigan's popular Upper Peninsula resort area.

It took the Copper Country residents some time to rediscover the thrill of live theatre. "The first four or five weeks of the season were disheartening," said Barry. "We did not have the time or means to advertise the Playhouse very widely, and some nights we played to audiences that were less than 50. We were about ready to throw in the sponge by August, but then it seems that almost a miracle happened. Our local residents began discovering that our plays were good, and the acting excellent. Tourists began telling others about us. When that happened, we knew we were here to stay." In 1958 the Playhouse played to some 10,000 people in Calumet and 2,000 more at its appearances in Marquette and Mackinac Island.

During the winter this business was in the hands of Theodore Pearce, vice president and resident agent of the corporation, and Miss Martha

"THE WIZARD OF OZ"

Eddy and James Wescoat, both members of the Playhouse Board of Directors. Pearce stated that the Playhouse as a Copper Country industry was important, as its budget for 1958 was more than $25,000 in salaries and funds spent locally. This did not include the money that was spent by the many tourists who were attracted by the theatre or who stayed over an extra day to see a play.[27]

With the loss of the Kerredge Theatre in 1959, the well-known Calumet Playhouse was the last remaining showhouse of plush, refinement in the Lake Superior, Upper Michigan, and northern Wisconsin areas. The death of the Kerredge through fire brought to an end the long entertainment career of a theatre which opened in 1902 and served the public for 58 years. The Calumet Theatre now loomed as something akin to a Copper Country Pyramid. Like the Sphinx of the desert, it is solitary, a gem which shines forth from the past to contrast with the shallow stage cinema houses of the present.[28]

The Keweenaw Playhouse Guild, Inc. came into being late in the fall of 1961 upon the death of the Keweenaw Playhouse Incorporated. The latter, a financially undernourished summer stock company owned by a handful of stock holders, had for four seasons struggled to produce plays and musicals at the Calumet Theatre. Though not a financial success, it was a success artistically, and it succeeded in embedding in a segment of the community a desire for live theatre and a determination to do something about it.

A series of meetings were held out of which came the proposal that a non-profit community organization be set up "to operate, conduct, and maintain a playhouse for the presentation of dramatic and musical productions, and to devote

"LILLIAN RUSSELL"

the income therefrom, without profit to it, to the objects of said organization, which shall be as follows:

a. To aid worthy students in apprenticing as actors and helpers in musical and dramatic productions; and

b. To arrange for and give musical and dramatic productions appropriate for the education, instruction, and literary advancement of the general public."

By the first of the year (1962), the Keweenaw Playhouse Guild had been organized and its officers and trustees had embarked on a drive to raise $12,000 to make the 1962 season a reality. By opening day, most of the money had been obtained, and it was with a great sense of achievement that the Keweenaw Playhouse Guild saw the curtain go up on its first season. 1963 found another year of continuing support, with Guild members as well as visitors and residents alike becoming more and more interested in the Playhouse. Funds were expended to secure scenery, costumes, properties, and performers who would bring to the Copper Country an impressive schedule of musical entertainment.

Following on the heels of 1963, the 1964 season proudly ushered in its bannerline of carefully selected productions. With the dedicated support of the people of the Copper Country, the Upper Peninsula's only professional stock company looked forward to an expansive 1965 season at the Keweenaw Playhouse which was held in the Calumet Theatre.

At the time of the play "My Fair Lady," with Leland Ball as the producer and director, held on June 9, 1964, the officers of the Guild were: Mrs. C. W. Stallard, president; Joseph A. Romig, vice president; Mrs. Robert R. Hagen, vice president;

This old piano is still in use and is in good condition. Courtesy of Jay E. Dupuis, Lake Linden, Michigan

David M. Monroe, vice president; Martha O. Eddy, secretary; Leonard W. Miller, treasurer; and Walter Dartland, counselor. Fifteen trustees were also listed.

On Tuesday, July 17, 1962, the Keweenaw Playhouse Guild presented Blanche Thebom of Metropolitan Opera fame in a Franz Lehar's immoral "Merry Widow." Miss Thebom returned to the Copper Country from triumphant performances all over the world. She had previously appeared in the title role of this great operetta and thrilled thousands. A news article stated that Lehar's music was beautiful and provided an appropriate setting for Miss Thebom's limitless talents. Paul Barry had written a new script and adapted the lyrics to more closely adhere to the original production of this great classic, while yet maintaining great appeal for the audience. Many of the songs from "Merry Widow" had become great classical hits; "Merry Widow Waltz" and the lovely "Vilia" were perhaps the best known.[29]

The Gogebic Range Tamburitza Group, made up of dancers and singers, appeared on the stage of the Calumet Theatre on Sunday, March 21st, 1971. The origin of the Gogebic Range Tamburitza Singers and Dancers went back to the summer of 1968 when Ironwood was about to have its first summer festival, and national groups were formed to portray in music, song, and dance the customs native to each nationality. Mike Pavlovich of Ironwood was chosen to be the chairman of the Yugoslav group. He was fortunate to have a large and interested turnout for this first meeting, and soon the group progressed into one of the finest in the summer festival. This group then decided to call themselves the Gogebic Range Tamburitza Singers and Dancers because its membership consisted of people from Ironwood, Wakefield, and Montreal,

ROSE COGHLAN

Wisconsin.

Their appearance marked the initial steps in reopening the theatre for stage productions and moving pictures. Under the guidance of the new theatre managers, Rudy Ucman and J. P. LaPierre, the Calumet area people were again able to attend stage performances, cooking schools, moving pictures, and various other activities. A thorough cleaning and decorating of the theatre had begun. The Building and Grounds Committee of the Village of Calumet, consisting of Arnold Rosendahl, chairman; Matt and William Hendrickson, were spearheading the project through the cooperation of the Concentrated Employment Program of the Michigan Employment Security Commission and the U.S. Department of Labor. Arrangements for this program were made by Mrs. Frances H. Eastley, the center director. Chairman Arnold Rosendahl said that several weeks were required to clean and make the much-needed repairs to the lobby, rest rooms, stage, and auditorium, after which the painting would get under way in order to present a "new look" to the general public.[30]

In July of 1971, the theatre was leased by the Copper Country Intermediate School District under the government's Title III program. It was leased for a year, with an option to renew, and James Boggio of Eagle Harbor, consultant to the school district, was named its executive director. J. P. LaPierre of Houghton was also hired by the school district as theatre manager. The enthusiasm was shared by village trustee Arnold Rosendahl and village president William Hendrickson. They wanted to restore the theatre to its 1900 condition, which was estimated to cost about a quarter of a million dollars. There were many sources from which funding could be obtained—governmental and private—supplemented by what the theatre could obtain through

A view of the first floor, with the first and second balconies. Courtesy of theatre manager Mrs. Gloria Coello.

its own earnings.

Proceeds from the offerings that were obtained went directly into the restoration of the theatre, with the first concern being the condition of the seats; almost all 1,200 of them were required to be reupholstered. Cleaning, painting, repairs, refurnishing, and the reinstallation of accommodations, facilities, and items of decor that won the acclaim of actors and audiences since the year 1900 were all to be considered as the work progressed. Replacing each of the lights in the house was a project in itself. There were originally 968 of them, plus those in the porte cochere at the entrance to the theatre.

The village council, which had given its full support to the project, was well pleased with the arrangements that had been completed. The village received $1,500 for the first year's rent plus the cost of heating the building. In the same structure as the theatre, above the village offices, was a former dance hall. This was planned to become a historic museum in conjunction with the theatre restoration.[31]

That year, the 71-year-old building had been designated a "historical building" and recorded as such in the National Register of Historic Places, according to an announcement made on Friday, September 17th, 1971, by Congressman Philip Ruppe. Previous to this date, the theatre had been represented in the registered sites of the Michigan Historical Commission, and this new recognition, according to the executive director James Boggio, "was wonderful news for the area and for prospects for furthering use of the theatre for cultural and social benefit to the community." The National Park Service, which set forth the criteria for historic places, had indicated that

Restoration work at the historic Calumet Theatre began when Doug's Painting of Laurium became the "main attraction." Towering scaffolds were erected to permit the firm's crew to reach the theatre's ceiling and arch. The painters applied shades of ivory, gold and red according to the architect's specifications and as the work progessed, the difference between the painted and unpainted areas was like that of "night and day." Courtesy of Peterson of the Daily Mining Gazette, Houghton, MI.

this distinctive honor and recognition was made possible through the cooperation of the Calumet Village Council, Congressman Philip Ruppe's Office, the Copper Country Intermediate School District, and Director James Boggio.[32]

This action allowed the theatre to become eligible for federal grants to aid in its restoration and to further the cultural benefits that could be derived from it. Funds were already being sought from the Michigan Council of Arts and the Michigan Historical Society. Also, three men on the Michigan Employment Security Commission's Work Incentive Program were painting and cleaning the theatre.

February of 1972 found the theatre department of the Michigan State University and the Copper Country Intermediate School District negotiating with the Village of Calumet. The happy conclusion was that MSU's theatre department would reopen the historic Calumet Theatre for summer stock during July and August of 1972. Frank Rutledge, chairman of the theatre department, stated that it provided them with a significant field experience for graduates and undergraduates of their university.

The new plan was designed to provide a valid summer stock experience at all levels. It called for the production of four plays—two musical comedies and two modern plays—plus tours of the theatre and scenes from plays from the period when the theatre was built. The MSU Theatre sent a staff of four faculty that was financed by the university. The student actors and apprentices were assisted by the Copper Country Intermediate School District and Calumet Village in providing the theatre and housing for the company. Local support was also asked, as this was necessary to make the venture an annual summer vacation.

Carpenter Tom Mottonen of Laurium applied joint compound to the new plaster-board ceiling beneath the theatre's first balcony. Mottonen was employed at the theatre throughout its restoration for general carpenter and repair work. Other workmen were hired through the job program of the Michigan Employment Security Commission. Courtesy of Peterson of the Daily Mining Gazette, Houghton, Michigan.

In addition to operating the theatre, the MSU staff provided workshops in June and August for students and high school teachers interested in all facets of the theatre. Paul Kimball, director of the Performing Arts Project for the Copper Country Intermediate School District, said that it was this aspect that especially appealed to the school district. James Boggio was happy with the continuing work of restoring the theatre to its former greatness.[33]

Early 1972 also found an ad in the local newspaper announcing that the Upper Great Lakes Regional Commission had approved a $30,000 grant. Congressman Philip Ruppe and Senator Robert Griffin obtained this grant and also stressed that other federal funds for this project would be provided by the National Park Service of the U.S. Department of Interior.[34]

The restoration was being done by the architectural firm of Johnson, Johnson, and Roy of Ann Arbor. In March of 1973, the bids had been let; local contractor Doug Kolehmainen of Laurium was the low bidder. Painting was soon started, with several articles and pictures appearing in the local newspapers. Ace Hardware of Calumet was the low bidder for the paint contract.[35] Both spray and brushes were used by the painters, the spray for the larger wall and ceiling areas and brushes for the more intricate work. The painters were working in two shifts and wanted to fulfill their contract in six weeks. The painters began their work with 180 gallons of paint, with more to be obtained later. Towering scaffolds were errected to permit the firm's crew to reach the theatre's ceiling and arch so that they could apply the shades of ivory, gold, and red according to the architect's specifications. As the work progressed, on-lookers were heard to say that the difference between the painted and unpainted areas were like "night and day."

Before the painting was started, carpenter Tom Mottonen of Laurium applied joint compound to the new plaster board ceiling beneath the theatre's first balcony. Mottonen was employed at the theatre throughout its restoration for general carpenter and repair work. Some of the men who worked on the restoration were: Doug Kolehmainen, Ray Schoos, Bobby Hodges, Ken Savela, and Tom Mottonen.[36]

The Michigan State University Department of Theatre returned in 1973 for its second summer. Opening in July, they had expanded their lineup of six entertaining plays and two additional children's plays. The company advertised their plays as live "come-as-you-are" entertainment to one of Michigan's most beautiful state landmarks. The season started with "Butterflies are Free," followed by "Night Must Fall," "The Apple Tree," "The Lady or the Tiger," "Passionella," "You Know I Can't Hear You When the Water's Running," "Love Rides the Rails," and "A Funny Thing Happened on the Way to the Forum." The season opened on July 17th and ran until August 25th with performances every Tuesday through Saturday. In addition to the regular season, they once more held a Children's Theatre.

The year of 1973 also saw the official historical marker erected on the Calumet Theatre site. The large metal marker is two-sided and has raised lettering. It occupies a central spot in the small, shady park adjacent to the theatre. The Calumet Village councilmen who dedicated the sign were Emil Primeau, Arnold Rosendahl, Frank Beatty (Village President), James Perko, and Arthur Sutinen. [Author's note: Yes, it was named the

"Calumet Theatre," but the sign says "Calumet Theater." See cover of this publication for the sign.]

In December of 1973, a special meeting of the Calumet Village Council appointed a new Calumet Theatre Advisory Board. Village President Frank Beatty announced that the board would coordinate all activities at the theatre and advise the Village Council on its use and maintenance. The persons appointed to the board were Dr. Donald Murtonen, John Ryan, R. D. Mechlin, James Bennetts, Robert Roy, James Boggio, Paul Kimball, and Frank Beatty. The Village Council also appointed two of its members to work with the committee, those being John Vertin and Ferdinand Peterlin.

With the completion of the restoration in the first phase of development of the theatre to be completed in the fall of 1974, it was decided by the council that the investment in the theatre should be protected and that the community facility be maintained and operated in the best interests of the people in the Copper Country. This meant that the programming in the performing arts be coordinated and managed by a citizen group.[37]

The Summer Stock Company of the Michigan State University started their third year in 1974. The plays for that season included "Man of La Mancha," "Plaza Suite," George M. Cohan's "The Drunkard" and "Gypsy." This was Professor Peter W. Landry's third summer as the managing director. He was familiar with the area, as he was a native of Ironwood. Everyone was satisfied with the response in housing the students and in the renovations of the Calumet Theatre. The energy crisis had also been uppermost in everyone's mind, but

Both spray and brush were used by the painters, the spray for the larger wall and ceiling areas and brushes for the more intricate work. The several painters worked in two shifts and had expected to fulfill their contract in six weeks. They began with 180 gallons of paint, but required more before the job was completed, according to the firm's president, Doug Kolehmainen. Courtesy of Peterson of the Daily Mining Gazette, Houghton, Michigan.

the management was optimistic on two points: the Calumet Theatre had traditionally been patronized by local theatre goers and citizens, and secondly they felt that the national trend would be for people to go to one spot and vacation there. This would avoid the week or two-week travel holidays of the old, plentiful gas days. Paul Kimball was again instrumental in arranging for the MSU involvement in Calumet through the Copper Country Intermediate School District.

This year, visitors would also find added comfort and beauty in newly upholstered chairs, plush carpeting, a remodeled lobby, and a new grand curtain. The restoration of the theatre to what it looked like when opened in March of 1900 had been described as well worth the effort, and it promised to be a source of great pride to residents of Michigan's Upper Peninsula.[38]

The $120,000 restoration project also allowed the installation of new carpeting, the rewiring of the electrical system, the regilding of the walls, the the replacement of the original lights. "The only thing we haven't been able to find is the large original chandelier, but we're working on it," said Paul Kimball. Details have not been forgotten, Kimball said, even down to replacing the railings and the wicker chairs in the balcony seats. It was later found out that the copper chandelier which had hung from the theatre's dome was destroyed by fire on November 28, 1918. This three-alarm fire in the theatre, though contained to the stage area, melted the chandelier.

The restoration did not come cheaply, so the Village of Calumet obtained help from the Michigan Department of Natural Resources, who contributed about $60,000, the Great Lakes Regional Development Commission $30,000, and the Michigan Historical

Society $10,000. The Michigan Department of Education came up with the rest through in-kind services and supervisory help. The restoration began in the fall of 1971 and was completed in July of 1974. Some exterior work still remained to be done, plus replacing the theatre floor and remodeling the third balcony.[39]

The theatre was a favorite of the performers, as it had a stage 60 by 28 feet and a height of 60 feet from the stage floor to the ceiling. The fly galleries are separated by 48 feet and are 30 feet above the stage door. There are eight dressing rooms under the stage, and four star dressing rooms—two on either side of the stage in an area over the box seats. The seating capacity is 1200, with 419 seats in the parquet, 400 in the first balcony, and 380 in the balcony.

The Detroit Symphony Orchestra, with guest conductors Sixten Ehrling and Richard Hayman, conducted a program for the 1974 Upper Peninsula Summer Music Festival. It was held in three northern Michigan communities during the week of July 7th. In Calumet, the Detroit Symphony Orchestra's Festival appearance was presented under the auspices of the Calumet-Laurium-Keweenaw Chamber of Commerce and Coppertown, U.S.A. with the cooperation of Michigan Technological University. Also involved were the Gogebic Arts Council in Ironwood and the Great Lakes Choral Society, Inc., of Escanaba. The entire Upper Peninsula Summer Music Festival was presented in cooperation with the Michigan Council for the Arts and was another phase in the continued expansion of the orchestra's activities throughout the state.[40]

The concerts were held on Tuesday and Wednesday, July 9th and 10th. The two conductors were well known, as Sixten Ehrling was the conductor

This scene came from "My Fair Lady," a show produced by students from the Calumet High School in May of 1977. Courtesy of Mr. Bruce Norden, Laurium, Michigan.

of the Royal Opera in Stockholm for 20 years and was music director of the Detroit Symphony from 1963 to 1973. He is recognized by many people around the world as this century's finest Swedish conductor. Ehrling was then the head of the orchestral department at the Juilliard School in New York, conducted regularly at the Metropolitan Opera, and maintained a full schedule of International guest-conducting appearances. He conducted the classical performances at the theatre.

Richard Hayman had conducted the orchestra's annual spring cabaret "Pops" series since 1970, and he was the symphony's principal pops conductor. In addition he was the chief arranger for the Boston Pops Orchestra since 1950 and had scored Broadway shows and done orchestrations for numerous motion pictures as well as having composed and conducted for many major record companies.

On Tuesday night, the conductors received a standing ovation and a thunderous applause that would not stop until Conductor Sixten Ehrling returned for an encore. The Calumet Theatre was filled to capacity on that Tuesday evening, the first of two concerts which were held in conjunction with the rededication of the theatre following its restoration and designation as a state and national historical site.

The opening night audience was treated to almost two full hours of flawlessly performed classical music, presented live to the Copper Country people, that would have won over even the most singular-minded devotees of rock and roll. True to its reputation for excellent acoustics, the theatre allowed the music to flow as Ehrling deftly wove each instrument's every note into a multi-dimensional portrait of sound. The evening was a hot one, however, as the summer's heat hung

This scene came from "My Fair Lady," a show produced by students from the Calumet High School in May of 1977. Courtesy of Mr. Bruce Norden, Laurium, Michigan.

over the old stone structure with a temperature of close to 100 degrees. Ehrling later said it was "murderously hot" for his musicians and himself as they performed in the glow of the stage and music stand lights.

Arnold E. Lack, Assistant to the President of Suomi College, delivered the rededication address and described the theatre as "inhibited sculpture or petrified music"..."a tribute to the artist...to the designers and builders." He noted that the duty of the theatre is to keep awake a sense of wonder in the world, to strive against a continual tendency of the world to go to sleep. He said that while science and knowledge reassure, art is meant to disturb. "Like religion, theatre is to comfort the afflicted and afflict the comfortable." "We rededicate this place and set it aside as a place where magic moments can and will happen, sometimes happy and sometimes nearly holy moments, when we can hit where we live....We rededicate it in the spirit of elegance and taste in which it was conceived. Like the man who deeply loves his wife, we look fondly at the Calumet Theatre and say: 'You're not getting older; you're getting better.'"

Lack went on to say that the audience makes up the ingredients for the future of the theatre, that the people must become the patrons. "We dedicate this theatre in recognition that some have had the happy notion that American's want theatre that is alive and well...so let this place be rededicated as a place where theatre can take reality by surprise and where the performing arts can nourish the souls of a people."

A heavy bronze rededication plaque recognizing those instrumental in the theatre's restoration was presented to Calumet Village President Frank Beatty

An overall view of the Calumet Opera House, courtesy of theatre manager Mrs. Gloria Coello.

by Richard Newman of Johnson, Johnson, and Roy Architects of Ann Arbor.[41] The proceeds from the symphony's performance was presented to the theatre by Coppertown U.S.A., the sponsoring agency for the concerts. Dr. Donald Murtonen, president of the Coppertown U.S.A. Development Corporation, delivered a check for $1,246.16 to Charles Stetter, chairman of the theatre board. The money was used for improvements to and maintenance of the theatre.

The Calumet Theatre ballroom was completely restored in 1978. This project represented the preservation of historic community facilities and a rejuvenation of cultural and artistic resources. The plan for restoring the ballroom, which adjoins the theatre in the Calumet Village Hall, began on July 5th of 1977 and was completed in February of 1978. A committee chaired by Mary Lewis met the task with a handful of CETA (Concentrated Employment Training Act) employees, a few basic tools, and limited funds. "The committee was especially fortunate to have the services of Chuck Aubin," according to Lewis. "Through dedication and special skills, Chuck recaptured the former splendor of the ballroom as it once was." Various other individuals and businesses contributed labor or materials, Lewis noted.

Milford and Sons Contractors of Calumet donated the use of their scaffolding for the duration of the project. Robert Mishica of Corona, California, provided boxes of supplies for refinishing all of the woodwork; John Vertin of Calumet donated antique ceiling light fixtures, and Ronald LaBonte of Marquette furnished the fire escape door and hardware at nominal cost. Phil Lewis drew up the architectural design for the fire escape, Ted Pentzold of Laurium and Alen Steck of Calumet collaborated on the color scheme for the room, and a number of local merchants contributed

Calumet Theatre

TUESDAY, EVE., JUNE 24

ONE APPEARANCE ONLY.

MR. RICHARD

MANSFIELD

- IN -

BEAUCAIRE

With Entire Company and Complete Original Production.

Free List Entirely Suspended.

PRICES

All Down Stairs	$2 50
First Two Rows in Balcony	2 00
Balance of Balcony	1 50
Balcony Circle	1 00
Gallery	75
Box Seats	3 00

SPECIAL TRAIN OVER M. R. R. R.

From Lake Linden, Dollar Bay, Houghton and Hancock. Reduced rates on railroad from Ontonagon, L'Anse, Baraga, Chassell and all intermediate points.

Seat Sale open Thursday at 2 p. m.

Cash deposit required on tickets held 24 hours after opening of sale.

Published in the Copper Evening News, Calumet, Mich, on Friday, June 20, 1902.

through discounts on the merchandise purchased.

Revenue sharing funds allocated by the Houghton County Board of Commissioners came to $9,300. There were also donations from private sources, Bicentennial ethnic groups, and by the Calumet Village Centennial Committee, which helped to meet the costs of installing the heating system, insulation, and fire escape. Periodically the project labor was reinforced by the Baraga-Houghton-Keweenaw Community Action Agency.[42]

During the early months of 1979, the local newspapers carried much news about the theatre and how it was to be run. The theatre was in much better shape financially now than it had been in years, according to Village President Rita Finch. Old debts were being repaid, and even the salaries of the people involved were being met. Gloria Quello, the acting theatre manager, had been improving its public relations program, establishing rapport with groups that had been alienated, and was now moving ahead.[43]

Gloria Quello was named the manager and Michael Berndt coordinator at a special session of the Village Council held on March 1, 1979. Mrs. Quello was a former office clerk in the village and had been handling the theatre business for several months, as Dennis Gorgas had left to accept a position elsewhere. Michael Berndt first became involved with theatre operations as a member of the theatre advisory board. His position as program coordinator was part-time only.

The theatre is now on a solid foundation, both physically and financially. It is this author's belief that with such people as Gloria Quello, Rita Finch, Charles Stetter, Frank Beatty, James Boggio, Paul Kimball, John Vertin, and a list of others too long to publish, that this theatre will continue to be a success and a pride to the citizens of the Copper Country.

REFERENCES

[1]The Daily Mining Gazette, Houghton, MI, March 20, 1900, p. 5

[2]The Daily Mining Gazette, Houghton, MI, March 21, 1900, p. 5

[3]The Copper Country Evening News, Calumet, MI, March 21, 1900, p. 6

[4]The Copper Country Evening News, Calumet, MI, March 21, 1900, p. 6

[5]Michigan History Magazine, Vol. XXVII, article titled "The Opera House as a Social Institution in Michigan," by Willis F. Dunbar, 1943, p. 669

[6]Boom Copper, by Angus Murdoch, republished by Roy W. Drier and Louis G. Koepel, 1964, p. 151 and 152

[7]The Copper Country Evening News, Calumet, MI, March 22, 1900, p. 5

[8]The Daily Mining Gazette, Houghton, MI, September 24, 1966, p. 1

[9]The Copper Country Evening News, Calumet, MI, December 3, 1900, p. 5

[10]The Copper Country Evening News, Calumet, MI, December 7, 1900, p. 8

[11]The Daily Mining Gazette, Houghton, MI, March 4, 1902, p. 5

[12]The Copper Country Evening News, Calumet, MI, March 17, 1902, p. 4

[13]The Daily Mining Gazette, Houghton, MI, March 15, 1902, p. 2

[14]The Daily Mining Gazette, Houghton, MI, May 30, 1911, p. 3

[15]The Daily Mining Gazette, Houghton, MI, May 31, 1911, p. 6

[16]The Daily Mining Gazette, Houghton, MI, June 1, 1911, p. 3

[17]The Daily Mining Gazette, Houghton, MI, October 2, 1971, front page

[18]The Calumet News, Calumet, MI, January 14, 1916, p. 8

[19]The Calumet News, Calumet, MI, January 19, 1916, p. 2

[20]The Calumet News, Calumet, MI, February 19, 1918, p. 2

[21]The Calumet News, Calumet, MI, September 23, 1919, p. 2

[22]The Calumet News, Calumet, MI, September 29, 1919, p. 8

[23]The Daily Mining Gazette, Houghton, MI, March 31, 1921, p. 6

[24]<u>The Daily Mining Gazette</u>, Houghton, MI, February 22, 1925, p. 7

[25]<u>The Daily Mining Gazette</u>, Houghton, MI, May 3, 1935, p. 11

[26]<u>The Daily Mining Gazette</u>, Houghton, MI, November 6, 1954, p. 2

[27]<u>The Daily Mining Gazette</u>, Houghton, MI, April 11, 1959, p. 1

[28]<u>The Daily Mining Gazette</u>, Houghton, MI, June 20, 1959, p. 1

[29]<u>The Daily Mining Gazette</u>, Houghton, MI, July 16, 1962, p. 8

[30]<u>The Daily Mining Gazette</u>, Houghton, MI, March 13, 1971, p. 5

[31]<u>The Daily Mining Gazette</u>, Houghton, MI, July 20, 1971, p. 13

[32]<u>The Daily Mining Gazette</u>, Houghton, MI, September 17, 1971, front page

[33]<u>The Daily Mining Gazette</u>, Houghton, MI, February 10, 1972, p. 1

[34]<u>The Daily Mining Gazette</u>, Houghton, MI, April 26, 1972, p. 6

[35]<u>The Daily Mining Gazette</u>, Houghton, MI, March 7, 1973, p. 2

[36]The Daily Mining Gazette, Houghton, MI, March 26, 1973, p. 10

[37]The Daily Mining Gazette, Houghton, MI, December 21, 1973, p. 14

[38]The Daily Mining Gazette, Houghton, MI, June 27, 1974, p. 9

[39]The Milwaukee Journal, Milwaukee, WI, part 2, Sunday, July 7, 1974

[40]The Daily Mining Gazette, Houghton, MI, June 8, 1974, p. 4

[41]The Daily Mining Gazette, Houghton, MI, July 10, 1974, p. 13

[42]The Daily Mining Gazette, Houghton, MI, February 22, 1978, p. 7

[43]The Daily Mining Gazette, Houghton, MI, February 16, 1979, p. 3

SOURCES

The references listed below were used in gathering information to aid in the writing of this publication. I especially used the resources of the Michigan Technological University Library and the Daily Mining Gazette, both of Houghton Michigan. I am indebted to Margaret E. Carlson, David H. Thomas and Robert D. Patterson of the Michigan Technological University Library for their assistance and the materials they provided from the Archives Section. Also many thanks to Mrs. Gloria Coello, the manager of the theatre who provided many articles, technicial assistance and much encouragement.

PUBLICATIONS

Michigan History Magazine, published quarterly by the Michigan Historical Commission, Lansing, Michigan

Boom Copper, by Angus Murdoch, 1964

A Pictorical History of the American Theatre, by Daniell Blum, (1900 - 1956), 1960

Michigan Through the Centuries, by Willis F. Dunbar, Vol. II, 1955

NEWSPAPERS

Copper Country Evening News, Calumet, Michigan

Copper Island Sentinel, Calumet, Michigan

Daily Mining Gazette, Houghton, Michigan

Native Copper Times, Lake Linden, Michigan

Portage Lake Gazette, Houghton, Michigan

Milwaukee Journal, Milwaukee, Wisconsin

ADD THIS COPPER COUNTRY LOCAL HISTORY SERIES TO YOUR PERSONAL LIBRARY

COR-AGO, A LAKE LINDEN MEDICINE COMPANY
First of a local history series

A COPPER COUNTRY LOGGER'S TALE
Second of a local history series

GREGORYVILLE - THE HISTORY OF A HAMLET LOCATED ACROSS FROM LAKE LINDEN, MICHIGAN
Third of a local history series

WHITE CITY - THE HISTORY OF AN EARLY COPPER COUNTRY RECREATIONAL AREA
Fourth of a local history series

SOME COPPER COUNTRY NAMES AND PLACES
Fifth of a local history series

THE HISTORY OF LAKE LINDEN, MICHIGAN
Sixth of a local history series

THE HISTORY OF JACOBSVILLE AND ITS SANDSTONE QUARRIES
Seventh of a local history series

THE HISTORY OF COPPER HARBOR, MICHIGAN
Eight of a local history series

THE HISTORY OF EAGLE HARBOR, MICHIGAN
Ninth of a local history series

LAKE LINDEN'S YESTERDAY - A PICTORIAL HISTORY VOLUME I
Tenth of a local history series

THE HISTORY OF EAGLE RIVER, MICHIGAN
Eleventh of a local history series

JOSEPH BOSCH AND THE BOSCH BREWING COMPANY
Twelfth of a local history series

COPPER FALLS - JUST A MEMORY
Thirteenth of a local history series

THE CALUMET THEATRE
Fourteenth of a local history series

EARLY DAYS IN MOHAWK, MICHIGAN
Fifteenth of a local history series

LAKE LINDEN'S YESTERDAY - A PICTORIAL HISTORY, VOLUME II
Sixteenth of a local history series

THE KEWEENAW WATERWAY
Seventeenth of a local history series

A BRIEF HISTORY OF AHMEEK, MICHIGAN
Eighteenth of a local history series

ALL ABOUT MANDAN, MICHIGAN
Nineteenth of a local history series

HANCOCK, MICHIGAN, REMEMBERED, VOLUME I
Twentieth of a local history series

THE SETTLING OF COPPER CITY, MICHIGAN
Twenty-first of a local history series

LAKE LINDEN'S YESTERDAY - A PICTORIAL HISTORY, VOLUME III
Twenty-second of a local history series

A BRIEF LIST OF PUBLICATIONS PERTAINING TO COPPER COUNTRY HISTORY
(This publication is not part of the series)